PROJECT: THE HUMAN BODY

Gyles Brandreth

Illustrated by
Rowan Barnes Murphy

Introduction by
Dr. Robert Lefever
MA MB BChir MRCGP
AR CH

This is the book I should have read when I was young
– but it wasn't written then, so I had to wait until I was
at university before I discovered how the human body
is made and how it works. It was never as much fun
for me learning it all the hard way as it will be for you
reading this excellent text, understanding the
diagrams and laughing at the cartoons. Even if you
don't want to be a doctor, nurse, or
other health worker, it is still a
good idea to know about
your own body. It's the only
one you've got, so learn how
it works, and then you'll
know how to look after it.

CORGI-CAROUSEL
TRANSWORLD PUBLISHERS LTD.

A CORGI-CAROUSEL BOOK 0 552 54139 7

First publication in Great Britain

PRINTING HISTORY
Corgi-Carousel Edition published 1978

Corgi-Carousel Books are published by
Transworld Publishers Ltd.
Century House,
61–63 Uxbridge Road,
Ealing, London W.5.

Filmset by Keyspools Ltd, Golborne, Lancashire
Made and printed by The Guernsey Press Co. Ltd, Guernsey, Channel
Islands.

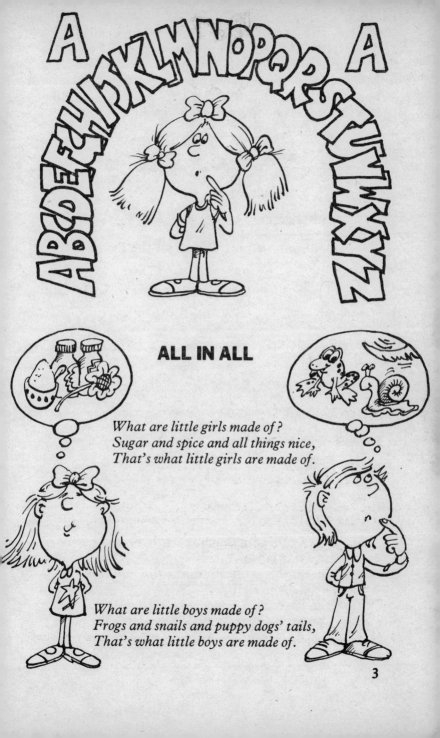

ALL IN ALL

What are little girls made of?
Sugar and spice and all things nice,
That's what little girls are made of.

What are little boys made of?
Frogs and snails and puppy dogs' tails,
That's what little boys are made of.

'**RUBBISH!**' you say and quite right too. But what are we all made of?

Well, we're made up—each one of us—of skin and bones, of muscles and nerves, of heart and brain, and of lots of obvious and not-so-obvious things besides.

In an adult there is:

enough fat to make two dozen big cakes of soap;
enough sulphur to kill all the fleas on a dog;

enough lime to whitewash a chicken coop;
enough carbon to make the lead for 9,000 pencils;
enough iron to make a solid nail;
enough water to fill a nine-litre tank.

Yes. But what makes up the skin and the bones, the muscles and the nerves, the heart and the brain, the fat and the sulphur and the lime and the carbon and the iron and the water and what have you. The answer: **CELLS**.

Our bodies are made of millions of tiny living cells. There are more than 50,000,000,000,000 cells in one human body and most of them are so small that you could fit 100,000 of them onto the head of a pin!

Each of the parts of your body that this book describes is made up of a mass of cells. They come in all sorts of shapes and sizes and when they are grouped together they are called **TISSUE**. The different parts of your body are made up of different kinds of body tissue. When different kinds of body tissue are organised to perform a particular kind of work the tissues form an **ORGAN**. When different organs work together to do a special job the group of organs is called a **SYSTEM**.

The systems are made up of organs. The organs are made up of tissues. The tissues are made up of cells. And that's what this book—and your body—is really all about.

5

BLOOD, BLOOD, GLORIOUS BLOOD!

Blood is often called '*the river of life*'. Certainly, the human body would be lost without it! Its work is vital:

– Blood supplies the cells of the body with water and nourishment.

– Blood takes oxygen from the lungs and carbon dioxide to them.

- Blood removes the waste products from the body's cells.
- Blood transports heat from the hotter to the cooler regions.
- Blood contains cells that fight disease and substances that can repair cut and bruised parts of the body.

Blood is made up of liquid and solid parts. The liquid part is called **PLASMA**: it is straw-coloured and counts for more than half our blood (some 55%). The solid parts are called **RED CORPUSCLES**, **WHITE CORPUSCLES** and **PLATELETS**. They are tiny.

The average adult body contains:
  Six litres of blood ($10\frac{1}{2}$ pints).
Those six litres contain roughly:
  25,000,000,000,000 red corpuscles;
  between 20,000,000,000 and
  50,000,000,000 white corpuscles;
  and 1,250,000,000,000 platelets.

RED CORPUSCLES, disc-shaped and concave on each side, contain a substance called **haemoglobin** (a compound of iron), and haemoglobin both picks up oxygen from the lungs and delivers it to cells in all parts of the body. Without oxygen, haemoglobin is dark blue in colour, almost black, but when it combines with oxygen it turns red, which is why the blood you see coming out of a cut is red.

(If you enjoy amazing statistics, remember that the blood in an adult human body contains some 25,000,000,000,000 red corpuscles and then marvel at the fact that there are about 280,000,000 molecules of haemoglobin in each and every red corpuscle!)

WHITE CORPUSCLES are far fewer in number, but most of them are larger than the red ones. They have no fixed shape and they move about by changing shape. Their main job is to help keep the body healthy by fighting dangerous bacteria. To destroy a bacterium a white corpuscle moves over it and eats it up. It may die in the process and go (with the dead bacteria) to form pus. When large numbers of bacteria get into the blood, the body automatically produces more white corpuscles to destroy the bacteria.

The **PLATELETS** form the part of the blood that makes it clot. If your blood didn't clot you could bleed to death with only the slightest cut. People who suffer from a condition called **haemophilia** have blood that does not clot quickly.

The **PLASMA**, which is more than half of the whole blood, is itself **91% water**. The rest of it is salts and proteins and what has been described as '*the blood cargo*', the nourishment, waste products and so on that are being carried around the body.

The **HEART** is the wonderfully efficient pump that moves our blood through the body. It is a muscle, about the size of your clenched fist, that contracts and relaxes about seventy times a minute. Each contraction and relaxation of the heart counts as one heartbeat.

9

2,500,000,000,000

Your heart beats about 100,000 times a
day.
In a year it beats about 36,000,000 times.
In an average lifetime a heart beats
some 2,500,000,000,000 times!

The heart, which is situated in
the middle of the chest slightly to
the left-hand side, is divided into four
chambers. The upper two chambers
are called **auricles** and the lower
two chambers are called **ventricles**:

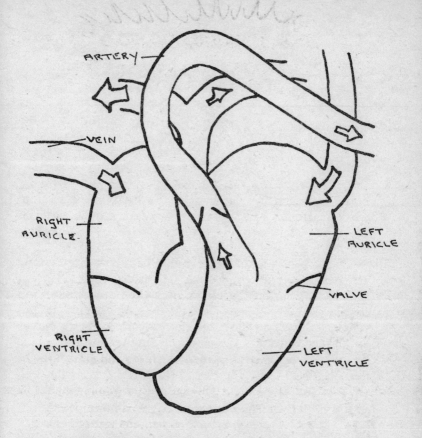

Each auricle is connected with the ventricle below it by a valve that allows a flow **from** the auricle **to** the ventricle, but not the other way round. When the right ventricle of the heart contracts, blood is forced into a large **artery** that leads to the **lungs. Arteries are the tubes that carry the blood** *away* **from the heart**. It's in the lungs that the red corpuscles collect the oxygen and get rid of carbon dioxide. From the lungs, the blood goes through the veins that lead back to the heart. **Veins are the tubes that carry the blood** *towards* **the heart**. The blood enters the left auricle and passes through the **valve** leading to the left ventricle. When the left ventricle contracts the blood flows into another large artery, which branches into smaller arteries which branch into even smaller arteries which branch into smaller arteries still!

The smallest arteries are called capillary arteries and are the finest tubes connecting arteries to veins. It is from the capillaries that the blood gives the nourishment and oxygen to the cells and collects the carbon dioxide and other waste. The tiny capillaries connect with larger and larger veins and the blood flowing through the veins finally reaches a large vein that enters the heart's right auricle. From the right auricle the blood travels through the valve leading to the right ventricle and so completes its trip around the body.

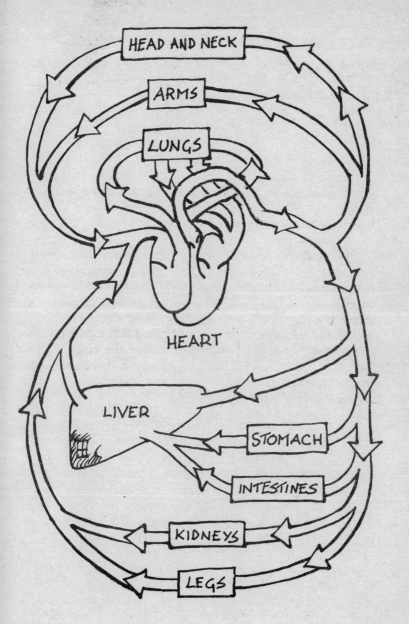

HEAD AND NECK

ARMS

LUNGS

HEART

LIVER

STOMACH

INTESTINES

KIDNEYS

LEGS

13

The round trip of blood from the heart to the furthest part of the body takes less than a minute. The circulation of blood through the lungs takes only six seconds.

Over a lifetime of seventy years the heart pumps about 250,000,000,000 litres of blood through the body.

1. How fast does your heart beat? As a rule the bigger the animal, the slower the heart-beat. For example, a mouse's heart beats between 600 and 700 times a minute, but an elephant's heart beats only 25 times a minute. Your heart-beat slows down as you grow older, so a baby has a heart that beats 130 times a minute, but the average adult's heart beats only 70 times a minute. Count your heart-beats. You can do it either by listening to your heart through your chest or by feeling your own pulse. To listen to your own heart you will need a stethoscope or you can listen to a friend's heart (and get him to listen to yours) by pressing your ear against his chest. You will hear a double beat: *lub-dup*. The *lub* is louder, lower and longer than the *dup*.

To feel your own pulse place a finger on your wrist here:

When you feel your pulse you will just feel one beat. Take a watch with a second hand and count up the number of beats in sixty seconds.

2. When you need lots of energy—for running or dancing or jumping about—your heart will beat faster and pump more blood around your body. When it is really pushed the heart can pump five times the amount of blood that it normally pumps! Count your heart beats after you have been resting for a while and then count them again after you have been running hard for a while. What's the difference?

CHATTERBOX

When you want to make a noise, this is how you do it:

1. You let air out of your lungs.
2. The air passes through your **windpipe**.
3. Your **vocal cords** are in your windpipe and they vibrate as the air pushes past them.
4. The vibrating vocal cords make **sound waves** in the air and your lips and tongue and teeth can break up or squeeze the sound to make it into words.

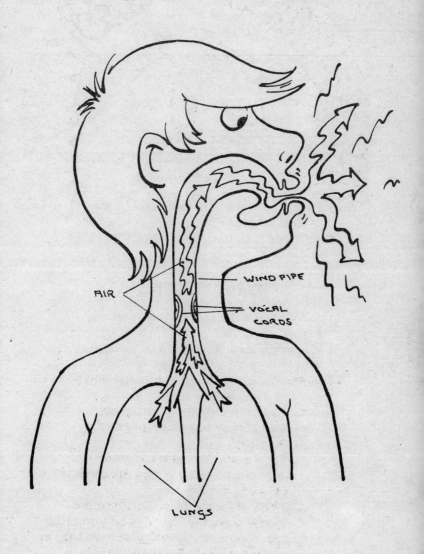

WIND PIPE

VOCAL CORDS

AIR

LUNGS

How high or how low the sound seems when you hear it is called **'pitch'**. The pitch of your voice, be it high and squeaky or low and deep, largely depends on the length and tightness of your vocal cords.

Both boys and girls are born with cords about 6 mm long and these grow as you get older.

By two they are 8 mm long and by six they are 10 mm.

A boy's vocal cords change more than a girl's.

At the age of fourteen, on average, a boy's vocal cords are 13 mm and a girl's are 12 mm.

At 20, a boy's are 24 mm and a girl's are 16 mm.

At 30, a man's vocal cords are 30 mm and a woman's are 20 mm.

Towards the end of your life your vocal cords will change again: but then, instead of getting longer, they will shorten and your voice, instead of getting deeper, will get higher.

PROJECT!

Most animals can make sounds and many can convey information in sounds, but none, not even the highly intelligent dolphin, use the voice in the way that human beings can.

The 3,000,000,000 or so human beings in the world speak some 2,000 different languages.

Mandarin Chinese, spoken by 550,000,000 people, is the world's most popular language.

English is the next most popular language, and is the mother tongue of 320,000,000 people.

Can you find out what are the world's twenty most spoken languages? And can you draw a Language Map of the World, showing in which parts of the world each of the different languages is most used?

DEEP BREATHING

The cells of the body need **oxygen**. You get oxygen from the air. In order to get the air from outside inside, we breathe in. This is how the system works:

1. To make you breathe in the muscle under your lungs, which is called the **diaphragm**, flattens down and your ribs swing up and out.
2. The pressure of the air outside your body is now greater than the pressure in your lungs, so that air is drawn into your nose, goes down your throat and windpipe, through a tube called the **trachea**, and then into your lungs.
3. The trachea divides into two parts. Each part is called a **bronchial tube** and each part enters a lung. Each

bronchial tube branches many times until the smallest branches are almost as small as the capillaries we met in **B** for **BLOOD**.

4. These tiny branches are called **alveoli** and the capillaries are in their walls. Oxygen passes from the air through the wall of the alveoli and combines with the red blood cells in the capillaries.

5. Carbon dioxide passes through the walls of the capillaries and into the air in the lungs.

6. When you breathe out, the diaphragm relaxes, the ribs move downwards and the air is squeezed out of the lungs along the same route it used to enter.

You may feel it must be your nose or mouth that start the breathing process, but as you can see it isn't. Breathing begins with that all-important muscle the diaphragm. In the past, when ladies thought they were being fashionable by squeezing their waists into corsets, they didn't realise that the tight corset prevented their diaphragms from working properly, which prevented them from breathing properly, with the result that all too often they fainted!

Sitting quietly and breathing normally, the average adult breathes about 7 litres of air every minute.

Breathing through your nose like this, the wind speed in your nose is 2 metres per second—which is the equivalent of a gentle breeze.

When you are involved in active physical work, the amount of air you breathe goes up to something like 100 litres in a minute.

This gives the wind speed in the nose equivalent to a really strong wind.

And, believe it or not, when you sneeze you can produce wind speeds as great as those in a hurricane or even a tornado!

PROJECT!

A normal adult, sitting down reading a book or watching TV, breathes in and out between ten and fourteen times a minute. Each breath lasts from four to six seconds. How many breaths do you take in a minute when you are sitting down? And how many do you take when you are walking and running?

Make a chart showing the different activities you are involved in every day and mark the number of breaths-per-minute by each one.

EAR! EAR!

As everybody knows, if you didn't have ears you wouldn't be able to hear. But did you also know that if you didn't have ears you wouldn't even be able to stand up? Hearing is the obvious job that the ears do for us. But they do an even more important and basic job as well: they help us keep our balance, they give us our **'equilibrium'**.

Inside the **inner ear** there are three semi-circular canals filled with liquid and two containers filled with minute hairs and chalky substances. The canals and the containers, the fluid and the chalk, are **'the vestibular apparatus'** and without them you wouldn't know whether you were coming or going, standing or falling—you'd really be living in what seemed like a topsy-turvy world.

VESTIBULAR APPARATUS

Giving us our balance is the all-important job of the ears. That doesn't mean that giving us our hearing isn't an important job too. It is a vital job: no one wants to be deaf.

The part of the ear on the outside of the head helps direct the sound waves into the ear, but only to a slight extent. The real job of hearing is done inside. Sound waves entering the ear strike the eardrum, or **tympanic membrane**, and cause it to vibrate. Touching the inner surface of the eardrum is a tiny bone, the **hammer**. The hammer connects by a joint to another little bone, the **anvil**. The anvil is jointed to a third bone, the **stirrup**. Below the stirrup is the cochlea which is a coiled up tube.

When sound waves make the eardrum vibrate, the eardrum makes the hammer vibrate as well. The vibrating hammer strikes against the anvil, which passes the vibration on to the stirrup. The stirrup makes the liquid in the cochlea vibrate and the vibration in the cochlea sets up impulses in the nerves that travel to the brain—and that part of the brain that deals with hearing understands those impulses as sounds. And you have two ears, both doing the same job, to help you work out where the sounds are coming from.

Sound waves are like invisible ripples in the air. You cannot see them, but you can feel them. The ripples travel at different speeds and these '**sound frequencies**' are measured in terms of '**cycles per second**'.

A good human ear can detect sound frequencies from 20 cycles per second to 20,000 cycles per second.

The sound of a man's voice is about 100 cycles per second.

The sound of a woman's voice is about 150 cycles per second.

The note middle C on a piano is 256 cycles per second.

20,000 cycles per second sounds just like a faint hiss to a human ear.

Dogs are among the small number of animals that can detect more than 20,000 cycles per second.

Sound frequencies are measured in cycles per second. Levels of noise are measured in decibels, named after Alexander Graham Bell, who also gave us the telephone.

**When you can just, just, *just* hear a
sound that's 0 decibels.
A whisper is 30 decibels.
Normal talking is 60 decibels.
A loud shout is 90 decibels.
Noise becomes really nasty at 120
decibels.
Noises greater than 120 decibels cause
pain and can damage your hearing.
From really loud noises it is possible to
lose your hearing altogether.**

Try these two experiments. The first will teach you about the balancing job done by your ears. The second is to do with hearing.

1. Spin round and round and round and round. As you spin round, the liquid in your ears is spinning round too. If you suddenly stop, the liquid will go on spinning round for a few moments. The spinning liquid will send a message to your brain, which because you're now standing still but the liquid is still spinning, will have the effect of making you dizzy. (Don't get carried away with this experiment: spinning so much that you fall over when you stop isn't good for you.)

2. Turn on the radio or put on a record or a tape recording. Now cover both your eyes and just one ear, but cover them well. Revolve a few times, then wander about the room. Try to decide where the sound is coming from. See if you're right. Repeat the experiment several times and you will be surprised by how often you choose the wrong direction. If you just cover your eyes, but listen for the noise with both ears you will find the right direction every time.

FOOD FOR THOUGHT

We are what we eat—and if we didn't eat and drink we'd die. We need nourishment and we get it from our food. And, what's more, the right nourishment comes from a range of different foods providing us with different things that we need.

We need **CARBOHYDRATES**. Bread, spaghetti, sugar and starch are all carbohydrates. Carbohydrates are a source of energy, though if we have too many carbohydrates, they turn into fat which our body stores making us fat.

We need **FAT**. Butter, margarine, lard and olive oil are all fats. Fats are another source of energy and, on the whole, a better source of energy than carbohydrates. Again, if we have too much fat the body will store it and it will make us fat.

We need **PROTEIN**. Protein is manufactured in the bodies of green plants, so when we eat green plants and animals eat green plants, the plant protein is changed inside us and inside the animals into muscle. When we eat meat, which is the muscle of animals, we also get protein through the meat.

We need **VITAMINS**. **Vitamin A** is important for general growth and for healthy eyes and skin. **Vitamin B** is important for general growth and for healthy nerves and muscles and for good digestion. **Vitamin C** is important for general growth, for good teeth and skin, and for fighting germs. **Vitamin D** is important for strong bones and teeth. **Vitamin K** is important for the liver and for making the blood clot.

We need **MINERALS**. We only need them in small quantities, but we need a wide range of them, two of the most important being calcium and phosphorus for healthy teeth and bones.

To be healthy and to grow properly we need a **balanced diet**, combining all the different things we need in the right proportions.

Almost certainly somebody sometime has told you that you eat too many sweets! Almost certainly they were right, because too many sweets, too much chocolate and too many cream cakes are **bad** for you! But in a week, when you are being sensible and not eating too many sweet things, what exactly do you eat? Keep a detailed **Diet Diary** for a whole week, making a note of everything—yes, everything— you eat.

At the end of the week, take each ingredient on the list and work out what you got from it—carbohydrates, fats, proteins, vitamins, minerals and all—and in that way find out how balanced your diet is.

Compare your diet with the diet of a friend and with the diets of adults you know, your teachers, your parents and your friends.

GERM WARFARE

Throughout your life your body is at war, fighting off the **germs** that are constantly attacking it. Once the germs have got inside your bloodstream, it is the job of the white corpuscles to trap the germs and destroy them, but the germs can be destroyed outside your body as well:

> Sunshine kills germs.
> Fresh air kills germs.
> Soapy water kills germs.
> Tears kill germs. Whenever you blink, tears wash your eyes.
> Clean sweat kills germs—but also sweat traps dirt, which is why we wash it off.
> Your outer ear contains wax and hairs to trap germs.
> Your nose contains hairs to trap germs.

Most germs get into the body through your mouth.

Once they are inside your system it becomes the job of the white corpuscles to lead the battle against them.

In your life so far your body has had to fight millions of different germs. You could never list them all. But what you can do is list all the **illnesses** from which you have ever suffered. Name each illness, and the year when you had it. Then find a medical dictionary and discover the **cause** of each illness, the **effect** it had on you and the reason you were eventually **cured**.

HAIR RAISING!

The average adult scalp contains 100,000 hairs.

Redheads have rather fewer hairs on their heads—around 90,000—and blondes have rather more—up to 150,000.

A hair on your head grows nearly 20 centimetres a year.

It would take you about six years to grow a head of hair long enough to sit on!

37

Your hair is dead, which is why it doesn't hurt when your hair is cut. The hair cells are pushed up from a live root, the hair **follicle**, beneath the skin. Every few years the follicle has a rest and the hair growing out of it falls out. The rest lasts some three to four months, after which the follicle revives and a new hair grows out. The daily loss of hairs from a full head of hair is between thirty and sixty individual hairs. Although we lose hairs every day, the follicles which grew the hairs aren't lost. They are just taking a rest and will be back in action before long. It is only with baldness that the follicles do not come back to life again and grow fresh hairs.

Our skin is covered with hair, but obviously it is the hair on our heads and, in the case of men, the hair on our faces that grows most quickly. In theory you could grow almost twelve metres of head hair in a lifetime, but because of the regular moulting of each hair follicle every few years, it doesn't work out that way. Since the cycle of a hair follicle lasts from one to six years, the maximum length of a hair is likely to be in the region of just under one metre. Longer hairs have been known, but not **much** longer ones!

Human hair may be dead, but it is still pretty strong.
A single hair can support a weight of 80 grams.
The combined strength of all the hairs on a man's head will support 100 adults!
(Please take this for a fact: if you try supporting a hundred friends by the hairs of your head, the hairs would be pulled out at the roots. The hairs are strong enough for the job: the roots aren't.)

Are you going to go bald? Well, if you're a girl, probably not—though women can and do go bald sometimes. If you are a boy and you want to know whether or not you are likely to go bald, look at your father's head and your grandfather's and, if you can get hold of the family photograph albums, look at your great-grandfathers' heads and their fathers' heads too. If you have a bald father and grandfather then the chances are that, one day, you too will go bald. Never mind: as Kojak once said, 'Bald is beautiful!'

INTO THE INTESTINES

What happens to the food you eat? You know where it goes in and you know where it comes out, but what happens to it in between?

1. When you take a mouthful of food you begin by chewing it with your teeth. In your mouth you add saliva to it and the saliva begins the 'digestive process'.
2. The food, munched up and with saliva, is now swallowed and passes into the food pipe called the **ŒSOPHAGUS.** This is a muscular tube that pushes the food down into the **STOMACH.**

41

3. The stomach has a muscle coat and it is higher up in your body than you might suppose: it is just below your breast-bone. In the stomach the food is churned about while digestive juices pour in from the stomach wall.

4. From your stomach the food moves on into the **SMALL INTESTINE** and this is where most of the digestive process takes place. The small intestine has a multitude of tiny projections on it. They are called **villi**. The digested food, which is just a liquid by now, is absorbed through the villi and passes into the capillaries that are inside the villi. Now the nourishment from the food is inside the bloodstream.

5. The remaining food passes from the small intestine into the **LARGE INTESTINE**. Water is taken out of the food here and is absorbed into the bloodstream. The food that cannot be digested moves on to the lower part of the large intestine, the **RECTUM,** and from there comes out into the world (and the lavatory!) through the **ANUS**.

SALIVA
GLAND

NOSE

MOUTH

OESOPHAGUS

STOMACH

DUODENUM

SMALL
INTESTINE

LARGE
INTESTINE

RECTUM

PROJECT!

You can swallow food standing on your head! Don't try, because it's neither all that easy nor all that good for you, but it's a fact. Food doesn't have to fall **down** into your stomach. It can travel **up** to your stomach too. There are many other animals and birds who can eat and drink with their heads down so that the food and drink has to travel **up** to their stomachs—

—but there are some creatures that can't. Find out the names of any animals and birds that can only swallow food and drink by lifting their heads up so that the food and drink travels **downwards** into their digestive systems.

JOINTS AND BONES

Every **bone** in your body (except for one) meets up with another bone. And the places where your bones meet and link up are called **joints**. Most of the joints are the movable ones that help you to do everything from getting up and running to bending down to touch your toes and wiggling them.

On this skeleton most of your most important movable joints have arrows pointing to them:

If you want to see how important your movable joints are, try keeping them all stiff for five minutes. You will find it difficult to move at all!

Not all the joints can move. In your skull, for example, there are eight bones that make up the part of the skull that encases your brain. It is called your **cranium** and the bones in your cranium don't move.

A SKULL

JAW BONE

A baby is born with about 350 bones.
As you grow older lots of the bones grow together to form larger, single bones.
The average adult has 206 bones in their body.
Some have one or two more, because their bones didn't grow together properly.
Others have one or two fewer, because the growing together system went a bit too far!
206 is the average number.

As your bones grow, you get taller, of course, but your growth in height is likely to stop by the time you are $16\frac{1}{4}$ if you are a girl, and $17\frac{3}{4}$ if you are a boy. Between your eighteenth and your thirtieth birthdays, you may grow another three, four or five millimetres, but that's about it.

Taking your skeleton from top to toe, there are 29 bones in your **SKULL**:

8 in the cranium
14 in your face
3 in each ear
1 in the throat

It's the one in the throat (the **hyoid** bone) that doesn't meet up with any other bone. It's the only jointless bone in your body.

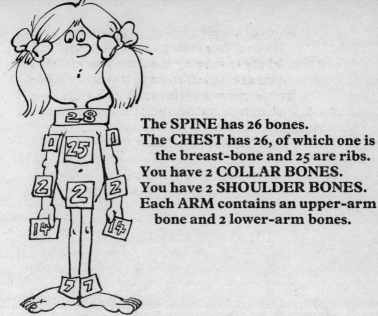

The SPINE has 26 bones.
The CHEST has 26, of which one is the breast-bone and 25 are ribs.
You have 2 COLLAR BONES.
You have 2 SHOULDER BONES.
Each ARM contains an upper-arm bone and 2 lower-arm bones.

There are 8 bones in your wrist.
Your palm has 5 bones, and there are 14 bones in the fingers of each hand.
You have 2 HIP BONES.
Each LEG contains a thighbone, a kneecap, a shin bone, and a bone on the other side of the lower leg.
There are 7 bones in the ankle of each foot.
5 bones are in the foot itself, with 14 bones in the toes of each foot.

If ever you are in bed and can't get to sleep, try counting all the bones in your body, starting with your toes. And if ever you want to prove to yourself that human beings have more useful bones than other animals, look at your hands and at the amazing things you can do with them. For example, try picking up a pencil or a cup **without using your thumb.** It isn't easy.

The bones at all the movable joints in your body are held together by tough, stringy tissue called **LIGAMENTS**. To help oil your joints and keep the movable bits moving a number of the bones contain a small hollow that produces a special lubricating liquid. The bones that meet up at joints that don't move are held together by a different kind of tough, springy tissue called **CARTILAGE**. Cartilage is what joins together the all-important bones of your spinal column and because it's springy it is a fairly successful shock absorber.

If you didn't have a skeleton inside you, your body would just collapse onto the floor like a wobbly blanc-mange. It's the bones of your body that give it its shape. The bones also help **protect** the softer parts of the body: the cranium protects the brain; the bony sockets at the front of your skull protect the eyes; the spinal column forms a tube of bone that protects your spinal cord; the ribs protect your heart and lungs.

Your bones provide shape, support and protection. They also act as anchor points for your muscles. What's more, the yellowish marrow inside your bones makes all the red blood cells. Your bones also help destroy old red cells, produce other ingredients for your blood and contain important minerals—like calcium, phosphorus, magnesium and iron—that keep you healthy.

So without any bones, you wouldn't just look like a jelly: you wouldn't be able to live at all!

1. Bones protect bits of your body **inside** your body. What would you look like if your skeleton was on the outside like a bony suit of armour? Design a skeleton to wear on top of the rest of your body— and then work out why the system we have now is so much more practical.

2. Of the 206 bones in the average adult body, each one has a name, and each name is something of a mouthful. For example, a medical student could tell you that the 31 bones in each of your legs have some splendidly tongue-twisting names: there's 1 **hip bone** (that's easy), 1 **femur** (a bit trickier), 1 **kneecap** (easy again), 1 **tibia** and 1 **fibula** (trickier again), 7 **tarsals**, 5 **metatarsals**, and 14 **phalanges**!

Find a medical textbook that gives you the names of all 206 bones in the body—and see if you can learn the names off by heart.

KIDNEY CAPERS

Grown human beings have two **kidneys**. They are about
11 cms (4½ inches) long, 6 cms (2½ inches) wide, 3 cms (1½
inches) thick and weigh about 141 grammes
(5 ounces). They have two jobs:

1. Blood goes into the kidneys to be
   cleaned. Clean blood goes back into
   the blood stream from the kidneys;
   the waste comes out of the body (and
   into the lavatory) as urine.
2. The kidneys regulate the amount of
   salt and liquid in the body.

If you want to find your kidneys, they are close to your spine in front of the twelfth ribs. While you are looking for them (and marvelling at the thought that over two pints of blood are pumped through your kidneys every minute), think about the name **kidneys**.

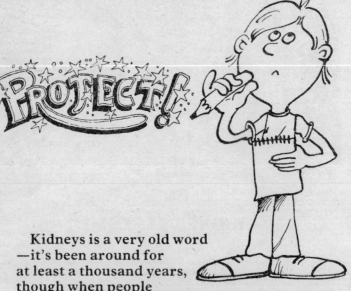

Kidneys is a very old word —it's been around for at least a thousand years, though when people first talked about kidneys they didn't know what part kidneys played in our bodies—and it's a very good word. It sounds right doesn't it? But can you think of a better word for kidneys? How about **KLEENBLO** or **BUBLUBU** or **POM**? Take all the main parts of the body and think of your own names for them. Start with everyday words—like **HEAD, NECK, SHOULDER, CHEST, HEART, LEGS** and so on—and then move on to more complicated words— **CAPILLARIES, INTESTINES, PLASMA, LIGAMENTS**—and see if you can invent names for different parts of the body that sound even better than the names they have already got.

LEFT-HANDED

Are you left-handed? If you are, you may like to know that there are roughly 200,000,000 other people like you in the world today. That's an awful lot of people, but it still amounts to only about five per cent of the world's population.

Of the nineteen out of every twenty people who are right-handed almost all of them were born that way. Some were forced to use their right hand instead of their left, which is not a good thing, and others had to learn to use their right hand when they lost the use of their left. (Horatio Nelson, on the other hand, lost his right arm and had to learn to write with his left.)

55

Way back in the Stone Age the number of left-handed people were about equal to the number of right-handed people.

In the Bronze Age, the number of right-handed people had greatly increased: only a quarter were left-handed then.

What is the explanation? Nobody really
  knows.
Some scientists have suggested that
  right-handedness increased when
  warriors began to hold their shields in
  their left hands to protect their hearts
  and used their right hands to hold
  swords or spears.
Can you think of any other explanation?

For an hour or a morning or even a whole day, reverse the work of your hands. Everything you normally do with your right hand, make your left hand do. And everything you normally do with your left hand, make your right hand do.

MUSCLE POWER

To move you need **muscles**. Your bones couldn't move without muscles to move them and in your body there are about three times as many muscles as there are bones.

Inside your body there are roughly 656 muscles and they are heavy.
About 42% of a man's weight is muscle.
About 36% of a woman's weight is muscle.

Muscles are made of bunches of muscle tissue held tightly together. Most of the muscles attached to your skeleton are linked to a bone either at one end by a **TENDON** or (much less often) at both ends. Your tendons can be very small or more than 30 cms long.

The muscles that move your skeleton are called **VOLUNTARY MUSCLES** because you can move them at will. But there are other muscles in your body, the **INVOLUNTARY MUSCLES**, that you can't move at will. In your eyes you will find a good example of the difference between voluntary and involuntary muscles: the voluntary muscles allow you to control your eyes to look wherever you want to look. But you cannot control the involuntary muscle that widens and narrows your pupils.

Muscles can only work by **pulling**. Even if you are pushing something as hard as you can, your muscles are in fact doing the job by **pulling**. By shortening and lengthening your muscles, you can make them bend or straighten your joints.

Feel some of your muscles at work.

1. Rest your right elbow on a table. With your left hand feel the middle or the top part of your right arm. Raise your right hand slowly, with your elbow still on the table, and

you can feel the muscle in your right arm
(the **BICEPS**) swelling up as you shorten it.

2. Put your left hand round your right forearm and drum your right-hand fingers on
the table. You can now feel your forearm
muscles at work.

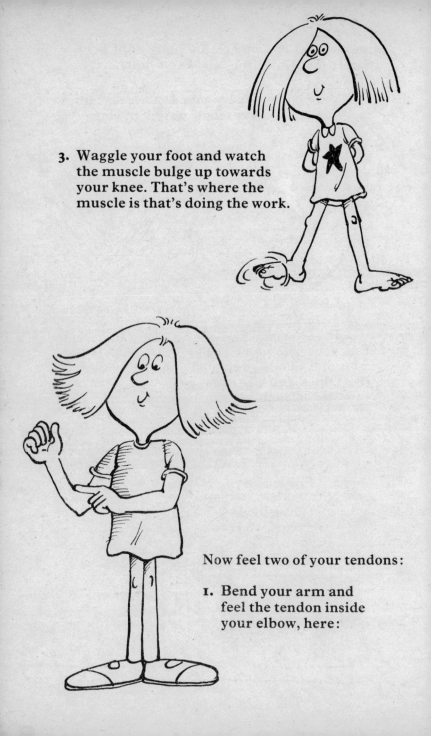

3. Waggle your foot and watch the muscle bulge up towards your knee. That's where the muscle is that's doing the work.

Now feel two of your tendons:

1. Bend your arm and feel the tendon inside your elbow, here:

2. The big tendon here steadies the whole weight of your body when you stand on one foot:

Feel how hard it is.

Take a close look at a piece of muscle. You don't need to cut yourself up to do: you just need a small piece of roast beef because **beef** is actually **muscle**.

With a pin pick apart a piece of beef. Separate it into long, thin strands. These are the fibres of the muscle tissue.

If you could look at a thin muscle fibre through a microscope, you would be able to see the muscle tissue made up of spindle-shaped cells.

NOSE JOB

First joker: My dog has lost his nose, you know.
Second joker: How does he smell?
First joker: Terrible!

If you had no nose you might still stink, but you couldn't smell. There is a small patch of special cells on the upper part of the inner surface of your nose and when the gases that float away from the things that have a smell come into your nose and reach that small patch of cells, the cells cause impulses to travel along the nerves to your brain and that's when you smell the smell.

Your smelling organ is more sensitive to some smells than to others. When you have a bad cold you may lose your sense of smell because the mucus that forms in your nose when you have a cold, covers the patch of sense cells and prevents the gases giving off the smell from coming into contact with the cells.

As well as helping you to smell, your nose cleans and warms the air you breathe. You breathe air in through your **NOSTRILS**, two tunnels that lead to a small cave inside your face. The air we breathe is full of germs and specks of dirt and the hairs inside your nose help to clean the air because the germs and dirt get trapped in the hairs. The sticky lining to your nose helps catch the germs and dirt as well. Tiny blood vessels in your nose also warm the cold air before it travels down your windpipe to your lungs.

PROJECT!

1. Give yourself a Smell Test. Close your eyes (or blindfold them securely) and get a friend to bring you lots of different everyday things that have different smells and see how many you can recognise. Without looking, sniff at a rose, some instant coffee, a piece of chalk, strawberry jam, a cauliflower, a teabag, a piece of wood, a pot of paint—and award yourself one point for every smell you got right.

2. When you have finished your Smell Test, you may think that your sense of smell is good. For a human being, it's probably very good. But by a dog's standards, your sense of smell is very, very poor indeed.

Over all, a dog's sense of smell is about a million times better than a man's!

If a dog knows his master, that dog will be able to recognise the master's smell on an old stick that the master has only held in his hands for a few seconds.

It doesn't matter how many people have handled the stick before or after the master: the dog will still know his own master's smell.

If you have a dog, set it some tests and see if it can recognise your smell.

OPTIC ORGANS

No, optic organs aren't musical instruments you find in churches. They're your eyes, the wonderful parts of the body that enable you to see the world around you—and read the words you are reading now.

A fully-grown human eyeball weighs about 7 grammes (quarter of an ounce) and has a diameter of slightly less than 2.5 cm (an inch).

A man's eye is a fraction bigger than a woman's—though it isn't as big as an eagle's eye.

(Birds have very large eyes for the size of their bodies: an owl's eyes, for example, take up one-third of its head.)

When a baby is born the size of its eyes is much nearer the size they will be when the baby has grown up than the rest of the baby's body.

Between being born and becoming an adult, your body increases its volume 20 times; your eye only increases its volume 3 and a quarter times.

One four-hundredth of a baby's weight are its eyes; one four-thousandth of an adult's weight are its eyes.

If you could look inside one of your eyes and cut across it, this is what you would find:

DIAGRAM OF THE EYE

TOUGH, WHITE COVERING

RETINA

IRIS

PUPIL

LENS

CLEAR LIQUID

OPTIC NERVE

Your eye is surrounded by a tough white protective covering. At the front of your eye part of this covering is round and see-through. Behind this see-through part of the eye is a space filled with clear liquid. At the back of this space is a circular tissue called the **IRIS** with a hole in it called the **PUPIL**.

The iris is the coloured part of your eye, and on the inner edge of it, around the pupil, you will find a ring of little muscles, all of them sensitive to light. In a bright light the muscles *tighten* and the pupil gets smaller. In a low light the muscles *relax* and the pupil gets bigger.

Behind the iris is a round see-through **LENS**. Muscles attached to the rim of the lens can make it focus on things that are near or far away. You are able to see things because light rays bounce off objects and travel into your eyes. In the pitch dark you can't see because there are no light rays reaching your eyes.

When a light ray passes through the lens in your eye it is turned **upside down** and **reversed from right to left**. After going through the lens the light travels through a small cave filled with clear liquid. All over the inside surface of this cave are nerve ends that are sensitive to light. The surface with the nerve endings in it is called the **RETINA**. The nerve endings link up with the **OPTIC NERVE** and the optic nerve takes the picture up to your brain. Your brain then turns the picture the right way up and the right way round so that you see it properly.

Each of your eyes sees a slightly *different* picture of the world. Look at an object with both eyes, then close one eye, then close the other eye (opening the first eye again) and you will see that the picture you get of the object looks slightly different each time.

Your brain joins the pictures you get from your left and right eyes together. With your two eyes working together you see better and you are able to work out how far or how near objects are. Put an object on a table, sit at the table and close one eye. Now try and touch the object. Do it ten times. You will probably miss the object a few times. With both eyes open you will probably be able to touch the object every time.

1. Watch your pupil shrink. Go into a very brightly lit room and stand in front of a mirror. Now cover up one eye completely for at least two whole minutes. Now uncover the eye and watch the pupil shrink! By getting smaller in a very bright light, the pupil protects your eye. By getting larger in dim light it helps you to see better.

2. See how you see better with two eyes. Stretch out your arms, like this:

Now bring your arms round and together so that the tips of your two outstretched forefingers meet, like this:

Do it with both eyes open and you will find that making your fingers meet isn't difficult. Do it with one eye shut and you will find it a lot harder.

3. Find your Blind Spot. At the point where the optic nerve comes into your eye, there is no retina, and so this tiny area in your eye is not sensitive to light. This tiny area, which is just below the middle of the back of your eye, is your **Blind Spot**.

To prove to yourself that you've got one, try this experiment. Look at these two letters:

A   **B**

Close your left eye and hold up the page in front of your right eye. Look at the **A**. Now move the page towards you and away from you until you find the point where the letter **B** disappears! At this point the **B** is focused by the lens of your eye exactly on your retina's Blind Spot.

PERCEPTION

Perception is turning what we see into something we understand. Our perception is *our view of the world*. Look at this drawing, and what do you perceive?

—a duck? or a rabbit?

You could perceive that picture in two different ways. It could be a duck **or** a rabbit. Generally, our perception of the world improves as we grow older and we learn to recognise more things for what they are. For example, a five-year-old looking at these two rows of dots will agree that there are the same number of dots in row **A** as there are in row **B**:

But if you showed the five-year-old these two rows of dots, he'd tell you that there were **more** dots in row **B** this time.

By the time you are eight or so you wouldn't make that mistake. You would be able to perceive that there were the **same** number of dots in rows **A** and **B** but the dots in row **B** were spaced out more.

Look at all the dots on the next page. They are all equally spaced, but they do seem to form patterns, don't they? The brain tends to group a mass of dots like these into different patterns. That's how we perceive them.

Sometimes we are the victims of **OPTICAL ILLUSIONS**, meaning that we perceive something to be so that isn't actually so. Our perception is fooling us!
See if you can answer these questions correctly.

1. In which of the two pictures is the moon bigger?

2. Of these three cubes, which one is nearest to us and which one is the largest?

3. Are any of these lines straight?

4. What's wrong with this triangle?

ANSWERS

1. The moon is the same size in both pictures. It just seems bigger in the second picture because it is nearer the ground, so we feel it must **be** bigger.

2. All three cubes are the same size, as you can see.

The background gives the impression that the third cube is larger and further away.

3. All the lines are straight.

4. The triangle is an **impossible** object. It can be drawn, but it can't be made. Look at the picture again closely and see if you can work out **why** you couldn't make the triangle out of wood.

QUICK-THINKING

The human **brain** isn't the biggest in the animal kingdom—it's a quarter the size of an elephant's, for example—but it is the best. Without it, you'd be lost for words—and everything else as well!

The brain is a soft lump of about 14,000,000,000 cells.
It weighs just over 1 kilogram (3 pounds) in an adult and occupies the upper half of the skull.

The largest part of the brain is the **CEREBRUM**. It controls your thinking in all its many aspects. At the back of your skull is the **CEREBELLUM**. It co-ordinates your muscular activity. The cerebellum controls all the voluntary muscles automatically. The involuntary muscles are controlled by a part of the brain called the **MEDULLA**, which is just at the top of the **SPINAL CORD**.

YOUR BRAIN

CEREBRUM

CEREBELLUM

MEDULLA

SPINAL CORD

The spinal cord goes down from the medulla through four-fifths of the length of your spine. Twelve pairs of nerves branch off the spinal cord and pass through the base of the skull into the brain. Thirty-one other pairs of nerves branch off the cord throughout its length. These nerves branch off to all the organs of the body, where they branch again and again, so that your nerves can carry orders from your brain to all parts of your body and can carry messages from your senses to your brain.

For example, if you dropped a cup and it breaks on the floor and you want to pick up the pieces, this is what happens:

1. When the sound of the cup hitting the ground reaches your ears, a message goes along the two auditory nerves to your brain.

2. When the messages reach your brain, part of your cerebrum perceives them as sound, and passes this information to another part of the cerebrum which recognises the sound.

3. This part of your cerebrum is your memory and it reminds you that the sound you've heard is of a cup hitting the floor.

4. The brain now decides to pick up the pieces. Your cerebrum now sends hundreds of different messages along the nerves to tell the many muscles involved that you want to bend over and pick up the broken cup.

PROJECT!

Your brain is the control room of your body. Different parts have different jobs to do. The **Cerebrum** receives the messages and stores them. The **Motor Cortex** of the Cerebrum controls the muscles and sends out signals. The **Cerebellum** co-ordinates, balances and sends the orders to the muscles you can control. The **Medulla** controls the muscles you can't control—your heart beat, your rate of breathing, the movements of your stomach and intestines, and many others. Instead of drawing your own brain as a brain, draw a picture of it as a military control room.

Here's Rowan Barnes Murphy's picture of his own brain at work:

What does yours look like?

RECORDS

1. HEAVIEST-EVER WOMAN: Pearl Washington—400 kg (62 st 12 lbs)

2. HEAVIEST-EVER MAN: Francis Lang —539.5 kg (84 st 11 lbs)

3. TALLEST-EVER WOMAN:
Jane Bunford—2.28 metres (7 ft 7 ins)

4. TALLEST-EVER MAN:
Robert Wadlow—2.68 metres (8 ft 11 ins)

5. SHORTEST-EVER MAN: Calvin Phillips —76.25 cms (26.5 ins)

6. SHORTEST-EVER WOMAN:
Pauline Musters— 58 cm (23.2 ins)

PROJECT!

Weigh and measure all your friends. Find out who is the tallest and shortest. Who is the lightest and heaviest. And keep a record of how people grow taller and heavier as they grow older.

SKIN TIGHT

The average adult is covered with about 8 square metres (eighteen square feet) of skin!

Your skin is—
> Airtight and waterproof.
> It protects your body from germs and from drying up.
> It helps to keep the temperature of your body even: when it's very cold, the blood vessels in your skin contract and force the blood deeper into your body; when it's very hot, the same blood vessels expand and bring more blood to the surface of the skin.

There are two layers to your skin. The top layer is the **EPIDERMIS**. It is made of dead, flattened cells, that are coming off our skin all the time. Below the epidermis is the second layer, the **DERMIS**, which is made of living cells. When the dead cells of the epidermis fall off the skin, cells from the dermis move up to the epidermis and replace them.

In the dermis are thousands of blood vessels and nerve endings—which is how you can *feel* things through your skin. You also *sweat* through your skin. Small tubes in the dermis open through the epidermis: they are your **SWEAT GLANDS** and the openings are called **PORES**. When it is hot the sweat glands make more sweat and as the sweat dries it cools down your skin.

When you are hot, more blood moves through the vessels near the surface of your skin so that the air can cool it. Colour cells in the deeper part of the epidermis give your skin its colour: sunlight can make those colour cells grow darker and the darker skin can protect your body from some of the sun's harmful rays.

When it is cold your surface layer of blood vessels shut

off and the deeper ones open up to help your skin keep in the warmth. This makes your skin look paler. The cold can make your hair muscles tighten. This releases a special oil, makes the hairs on your body stand up and makes goose pimples on your skin.

Build up a finger-print collection. The pattern of the skin on everybody's body is slightly different. Take all your friends' fingerprints and study the differences.

TEETH TIME

Here's a mouth full of **teeth**:

94

There are thirty-two teeth there, because the mouth belongs to an adult. Everyone has two sets of teeth in their lifetime. In the first set, which they grow as babies and young children, they have just 20 teeth. In the second set, which they grow as they get older and the first set of teeth fall out, they have 32. (Some people, who lose their second set of teeth, have a third set—but they don't grow them: they have them made for them by the dentist!)

Look at the adult teeth again.

There are 8 teeth called **INCISORS**.
They chop the food at the front of
your mouth.
There are 20 teeth called **MOLARS**.
They grind the food so that you can
digest it properly.
And there are 4 fangs called **CANINES**.
Dogs use their fangs to tear meat and
gnaw bones, but human beings don't
make much use of theirs.

Teeth go bad because liquid from chewed food sticks to them and makes holes in them. The germs in the air make the holes deeper and they become **CAVITIES**. The dentist fills the **CAVITIES** with **FILLINGS** so that germs can't live in the cavities. If germs are allowed to live in the cavities, your teeth will be ruined and will fall out.

British schoolchildren, from the ages of 5 to 17, have about 9,500,000 fillings put into their teeth every year!
And what's even worse, they have to have about 1,500,000 of their permanent teeth removed. They will never grow again.

That's why cleaning your teeth and gums regularly is **so** important.

When you clean your teeth you almost certainly use a toothbrush and toothpaste—but there are millions of people around the world who clean their teeth, but don't use a toothbrush or toothpaste. So how do **they** clean their teeth? Try to find out the different ways in which people—particularly in Africa, South America, India and the Far East—clean their teeth.

UGH!

'Ugh!' you think when you taste something you don't like—but how do you know that you don't like the taste? Well, your **TASTE BUDS** tell you.

Your taste buds are just below the surface of your tongue and in three different places in your throat. There are four tastes that you can detect through your taste buds—**SALTY, SWEET, SOUR** and **BITTER**—and you detect the different tastes in different places:

The taste buds at the *side* and *tip* of your tongue detect saltiness. The buds at the *tip* of your tongue detect sweetness too. Those at the *side* detect sourness and the ones at the *back* detect bitterness—which is why you often don't notice a bitter taste until you are about to swallow, when it's almost too late to spit it out! You have about 3,000 taste buds in all, but almost none of them are in the middle of your tongue.

Sweet, sour, salt and bitter are the only things you can taste through taste buds. You think you can taste lots of other things as well, but you can't. You **smell** them. When it comes to recognising the flavours of food, your sense of smell plays the most important part. Without a sense of smell, you wouldn't even be able to taste an onion! And when you have a cold and can't smell, the only taste you will recognize are the four your taste buds detect for you.

Nobody knows exactly how the taste buds work. Scientists are investigating how our senses of taste and smell operate, but they still have a lot to learn. Since trained scientists still have not discovered all the secrets of the taste buds, you would find working out how the taste buds work a very, very, big project—the work of a lifetime, probably.

If you can't spare a lifetime, play the Taste Buds Game instead. Blindfold your friends and give each of them different things to taste. Give **SALTY** things to one (salty ham, for example), **SWEET** things to another (sugar, for example), **SOUR** things to another (lemon juice, for example) and **BITTER** things to another (orange peel, for example).

When they have each recognised the tastes you gave them, get them to tell you the position of the taste buds that detected the taste for them.

VOCABULARY

Doctors and scientists use all sorts of complicated words to describe different parts of the body. Here is a list of all the unusual words used in this book. If there are any of the words in the list that you don't recognise, or that you recognise but can't remember what part they play in your body, see the letter by the word. Turn to that letter in the book and find out about the word.

Alveoli	D	Blood	B
Anvil	E	Bone	B
Anus	I	Brain	Q
Arms	J		
Artery	B		
Auricles	B	Canines	T
		Carbohydrates	F
		Cartilage	J
Balanced diet	F	Cavities	T
Biceps	M	Cells	A
Blind Spot	O	Cerebellum	Q

Stomach	I
Sweat glands	S
System	A
Taste-buds	U
Teeth	T
Tendon	M
Tissue	A
Trachea	D
Tympanic membrane	E
Valve	B
Vein	B

Ventricles	B
Vestibular apparatus	E
Villi	I
Vitamins	F
Vocal cords	C
Voluntary muscles	M
White corpuscles	B
Windpipe	B
X-ray	X

Write your own **Dictionary of the Human Body.** Take each one of the words in the list above and write a short description of what the word means and what it does. And if you come across other words that aren't in the list that you don't understand, find out what they mean too.

WHAT GOES WHERE?

1. Here is an outline of a human body. Inside the outline draw all your eating machinery—your mouth, your throat, your oesophagus, your stomach, your liver, your intestines—and see if you remember all the bits and can put them in the right place.

Now look at page 109 and see how well you've done.

2. Here is another outline. Inside this one, draw all your breathing machinery—your windpipe, your diaphragm, your lungs, your rib cage—and see if you can put all the bits in the right places.

Now look at page 110 and see how well you've done.

3. Here is a third outline. Inside this one put your heart and your main blood vessels. (You haven't forgotten that the ones leading out of the heart are called arteries and the ones leading in are called veins, have you?) Make sure you have blood circulating to your head and brain, your stomach and intestines, your lungs and liver and kidneys, and the rest of your body.

Now look at page 111 and see how well you've done.

4. Here's one last outline. Draw a skeleton inside it and make it as accurate as you can.

Now look at page 112 and see how well you've done.

WHAT WENT WHERE

1. The eating machinery.

2. The breathing machinery.

3. The heart and the main blood vessels.

4. The skeleton.

PROJECT!

Here is one more outline. Into this one put a newly designed inside for your body. Relocate the different vital organs—the digestive system, the respiratory system, the heart, the brain, the lot—and try to come up with a new inside that you think will work **better** than the one you've got.

X-RAYS

X-rays are a form of radiation, like light and heat. They are invisible and they travel in straight lines at the speed of light, 136,000 m.p.h. They can penetrate very thick material (up to 11 inches of solid steel) and have no difficulty penetrating the human body.

Although the X-rays are invisible, if they are directed at a special screen, the material on the screen will make the X-rays glow. So that if you put your foot in front of the screen, the shadow of your foot would be cast on the screen with the bones inside your foot casting an even deeper shadow.

PROJECT!

X-rays are used like this by doctors to examine the insides of people (and, in some instances, to help them cure diseases). Can you imagine twenty-five other rays, like X-rays, but doing different work? Take each letter of the alphabet and invent a ray for it. You might even invent a ray that could help show us the way our taste buds work!

Messages travel to and from your brain through your nerves. From your brain the main path they take is along the **SPINAL CORD**. The main nerves connect with the spinal cord and tiny nerves join up with the bigger ones:

BRAIN

SPINAL CORD

NERVES

We are made aware of the world we live in by our ten senses. Five of them are ones that people believed for hundreds of years were our only **senses**:

SIGHT
HEARING
TOUCH
SMELL
TASTE

Scientists have added the extra five to the list:

PRESSURE
HEAT
COLD
PAIN
PROPRIOCEPTION★

The nerves take the messages from the sense organs to the brain. The nerves that do this work are called **SENSORY NERVES.** When you stub your toes, nerve endings in your toes send the message of pain up to your brain. Your brain **understands** that it is pain, but you actually **sense** the pain in your toes.

★This is your 'positional sense' that enables you, for example, to know where your finger is pointing even with your eyes shut.

When the brain sends orders out to the body the nerves it uses to carry these orders are called the **MOTOR NERVES**.

Sometimes you react to something without having to think about it and send messages to the brain in the normal way. For example, if you put your hand on a boiling kettle, you will pull it away at once. Your automatic action is called a **REFLEX ACTION**. With a reflex action, the messages take a special short-cut, so that you react automatically and immediately. The reflex action makes you draw your hand away from the hot kettle straightaway. At the same time, the message telling your brain to feel pain is travelling through the **SENSORY NERVES** to the brain.

Test one of your reflexes just as a doctor does. Sit down and cross your right leg over your left leg like this:

Feel just below the kneecap of your right leg for the tendon that runs down from the kneecap. With the edge of your hand (or a ruler) strike the tendon sharply. Your right leg will jump upwards. You can't stop it. You don't need to think about it. It's a reflex action.

Do it a few times and you may find that your leg begins to move **before** you actually feel the sensation of your hand (or the ruler) hitting your knee!

ZZZzzzzzz

To live at all you need air and food and drink and **sleep**. Believe it or not, you need sleep as much as you need food. A normal human being will die quicker without sleep than he will without food.

While elephants and dolphins can sleep for just two hours out of every 24, the average length of a night's sleep among adult human beings is 7 hours and 36 minutes. Children sleep much longer and need to. People in their fifties take less sleep than people in their twenties, but people in their sixties get more sleep than at any time since childhood. On the whole, adult men sleep about ten minutes longer than adult women.

Make a **Sleep Chart**. Record the number of hours that you and each member of your family sleeps. Compare your family's Sleep Chart with the Sleep Charts of your friends. Good night.

PROJECT: CASTLES AND HISTORIC HOUSES   50p
by Gyles Brandreth   Non-fiction
552 54121 4

Would you like to meet the Kings and Queens of England or join
the quest for King Arthur? Have you ever been to a Haunted
House or discovered Hidden Passages?

If you like excitement, mystery and adventure you will certainly
like the castles and historic houses of England, Wales, Scotland
and Ireland. Discover and enjoy them with this special PROJECT
BOOK. It's packed with entertaining ideas and fascinating facts
about the strange and ancient buildings of your countryside.

PROJECT: NUMBER FUN
by Gyles Brandreth   65p
552 54138 9   Non-fiction

It's absolutely amazing the things you can do with numbers and
that numbers can do to you! You can turn yourself into an
amazing mind-reader, conjure up mystical magic squares and
curves out of straight lines! You can even make your calculator
giggle as well as multiply.

Filled with knotty numbers, stupendous sums and mind-boggling
mathematics — crammed with games and riddles and projects to
tease you — NUMBER FUN is fantastic fun!

THE BIG BOOK OF SECRETS
by Gyles Brandreth   50p
552 54123 0   Non-fiction

What kind of spy would you like to be? A deadly secret agent, a
courier, a dastardly double agent, a contact, a shadow? Do you
know who the Master Spy is? Could it be you?

This spy's handbook will tell you how to hide your equipment,
disguise yourself, make drops and pick-ups with your contact,
and send secret codes and ciphers. But be warned—keep this to
yourself — you never know who is listening . . .

THE DAFT DICTIONARY
by Gyles Brandreth   50p
0 552 54128 1   Non-fiction

Did you know that 'apricots' were beds for baby monkeys and 'kindred' was a fear of being visited by relatives? Have you heard that 'fleece' are insects that get into your wool if you don't wash properly and a 'dentist' is someone who always looks down in the mouth!

These and over a hundred other dotty definitions can be found in THE DAFT DICTIONARY — the most useless dictionary in the world!

JOKES! JOKES!! JOKES!!! A JOKE FOR EVERY DAY OF THE YEAR
by Gyles Brandreth   60p
552 54134 6   Non-fiction

A super, fun-packed book, chock full of zany jokes, puns and riddles — 365 of them to be exact — one for every day of the year! There's an International Gooseberry Month, a Horrid Riddle of the Week even a National Gigglers Week, and there's space for you to write in your own joke of the day too!

It's hours, days, weeks, months of fun — it's JOKES! JOKES!! JOKES!!!

THE GREAT BIG FUNNY BOOK
by Gyles Brandreth   £1.95
552 98045 5   Fiction

THE GREAT BIG FUNNY BOOK presents the funniest theatre show on earth, starring that most talented, stage struck tabby cat — SUPERPUSS!

Guffaw, giggle and gasp along with the audience as SUPERPUSS clowns his way through restaurants, hotels, hospitals and laboratories; boxing rings, barber shops, dentists and circus rings; darkest jungles, elephants . . . Among a brilliant cast of thousands — a special mention must be made for Leofric of Limerick, Master of Ceremonies; Down Boy, SUPERPUSS' loyal dog and companion; and Her Majesty the Queen.

Rich with riddles, puns and jolly jests — this is a show that you just can't miss!

If you would like to receive a newsletter telling you about our new children's books, fill in the coupon with your name and address and send it to:

Gillian Osband,
Transworld Publishers Ltd,
Century House,
61-63 Uxbridge Road, Ealing,
London, W5 5SA

Name ....

Address ....

....

....

CHILDREN'S NEWSLETTER

All the books on the previous pages are available at your bookshop or can be ordered direct from Transworld Publishers Ltd., Cash Sales Dept., P.O. Box 11, Falmouth, Cornwall.

Please send full name and address together with cheque or postal order—no currency, and allow 22p per book to cover postage and packing (plus 10p each for additional copies).